COUNTRY

Formal Name: Republic of India (The official, Sanskrit name for India is Bharat, the name of the legendary king in the *Mahabharata*).

Short Form: India.

Term for Citizen(s): Indian(s).

Capital: New Delhi (formally called the National Capital Territory of Delhi).

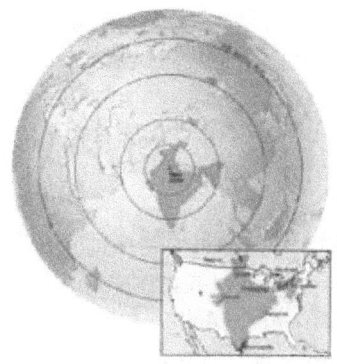

Click to Enlarge Image

Other Major Cities: India has 35 cities and urban agglomerations with more than 1 million persons. The most populous cities are Mumbai (Bombay) with 16.4 million people, Kolkata (Calcutta, 13.2 million), New Delhi (12.8 million), Chennai (Madras, 6.4 million), Bangalore (5.7 million), Hyderabad (5.5 million), and Ahmadabad (4.5 million).

Date of Independence: Proclaimed August 15, 1947, from Britain.

National Public Holidays: Makar Sakranti (January 14); Republic Day (signing of national constitution, January 26); Id-ul-Juha (movable date); Muharram (Islamic New Year, movable date); Holi (movable date in March); Ramnavami (birthday of Rama, movable date in March or April); Mahavir Jayanti (Birthday of Mahavir, movable date in April); Good Friday (movable date in March or April); Milad un Nabi (birthday of Prophet Muhammad, movable date); Buddha Poornima (birthday of Buddha, movable date in April or May); Independence Day (August 15); Mahatma Gandhi's Birthday (October 2); Dussehra (also known as Vijaya Dashmi, movable set of 10 days in September or October); Deepawali (also known as Diwali, movable set of five days in October or November); Id-ul-Fitr (end of Ramadan, movable date); Guru Nanak Jayanti (Birthday of Guru Nanak, November 26); Christmas Day (December 25). Many of these holidays are observed only by particular religions or in specific regions. The three holidays that are observed nationwide are Republic Day, Independence Day, and Mahatma Gandhi's Birthday.

Flag:
India's national flag has three horizontal bands. The upper band is orange/saffron in color, the lower is green, and the middle is white with a 24-spoke dark blue wheel in its center. The saffron symbolizes courage, sacrifice, and renunciation; the white represents purity and truth; and the green signifies faith and fertility. The wheel is the Dharma Chakra, an ancient Buddhist symbol used by the Indian king Ashoka to represent a "wheel of law."

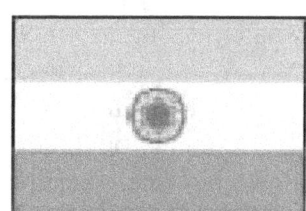

Click to Enlarge Image

HISTORICAL BACKGROUND

Early Empires: Whereas human settlement in India dates back to roughly 400,000 to 200,000 B.C., extensive urbanization and trade appear to have begun in the Indus River Valley around 3000 B.C. with the Harappan civilization. From this period until the termination of British colonial rule in 1947, numerous empires ruled various portions of South Asia, often assimilating a rich array of peoples and each adding its own contribution to an increasingly rich tapestry of cultures, ideas, and technologies. Indeed, many of India's current political, cultural, and economic traits have been influenced by historical events and trends, many of which pre-date European contact.

Among the most influential early empires were the Aryans, who migrated from Persia to northwestern India around 2000 B.C. and brought a new pantheon of anthropomorphic gods, an early form of Sanskrit language, a tiered social system essentially based on ethnicity and occupation, and religious texts that are an important part of living Hindu traditions.

From 326 B.C. to around 200 B.C., the Mauryan Empire emerged as India's first imperial power and ruled its areas with a highly centralized and hierarchical administration. For the next few hundred years, North and South India experienced a succession of ruling powers. From 320 A.D. to 550 A.D., most of North India was ruled by the Gupta Empire, which in contrast to the Mauryan Empire maintained a decentralized form of government, using numerous regional and local officials to govern vast territories with an array of local political, economic, and social arrangements. As under the Aryans, Gupta authority was religiously legitimized, and it was in this period called the Classical Age that the multiple components of Hindu culture became crystallized into a more unified system of thought.

From the disintegration of the Gupta Empire to the mid-thirteenth century, various regional kingdoms emerged, and conflicts among them often led to their defeat but rarely to their total annihilation. As a result, no highly centralized government emerged in South India, and South Indian villages and districts enjoyed much greater local autonomy than those in North India. During this period, South India engaged in flourishing trade with Arabs and Southeast Asia, which facilitated the diffusion of Indian mathematical concepts to the Middle East and Indian art, literature, and social customs to Southeast Asia.

Islamic influence in South Asia emerged around 711 as Arabs conquered part of Sindh (now in Pakistan), and by the tenth century Punjab came under the control of Turkic ruler Mahmud of Ghazni. By the thirteenth century, much of India had been periodically conquered, but rarely held for long, by a steady succession of Turkic rulers collectively referred to as the Delhi Sultanate or Mughal emperors. The most prominent Mughal ruler was the astute and religiously tolerant Akbar, who ruled from 1556 to 1605. Akbar oversaw substantial political and geographic consolidation by using locally established warriors and powerful *zamindar* landlords to control local populations and collect revenues. But over time, the administrative capacities of later Mughal rulers suffered from bloated and excessively corrupt bureaucracies and huge, unwieldy armies.

European Influence: European economic competition in India began soon after the Portuguese arrived in 1498, and by the early 1600s it was manifested in the establishment of commercial companies, such as England's East India Company, that attempted to capture the spice trade. In order to gain competitive advantages over each other, European powers also engaged in commercial and administrative alignments with Mughal power holders. By the late eighteenth century, the British had defeated French and Mughal forces to become the preeminent military and economic power in India.

The British used Indian assistance in various commercial and military matters, which enabled upward mobility for some Indians. The British also adopted numerous local economic and political arrangements that were established by the Mughals, and this practice maintained and exacerbated various forms of social stratification. A major turning point in the colonial occupation occurred with the Indian-led Sepoy Rebellion of 1857 to 1858, which seriously threatened British rule and led to a marked shift in colonial attitudes and practices. Although the British made some legal and administrative adjustments to placate Indians, colonial attitudes toward Indians shifted from cultural engagement—albeit to change Indians with Western ideas and technology—to insularity and xenophobia.

Independence Movement: By the 1920s, various Indian groups became active in attempting to end colonial rule, and the Indian National Congress Party, which had been established in 1885, eventually became the most prominent. Led by Mohandas Gandhi and Jawaharlal Nehru, the Congress Party promoted non-violence and self-sufficiency and thus garnered respect and support among both Indians and some British. But the Congress Party generally failed to attract Muslims, who often felt culturally and physically threatened by Hindus, and in 1906 the All-India Muslim League was established. The British periodically jailed Congress Party leaders for their social movement activities, but among the increasingly restive Indian population the British found Congress to be an easier group with which to negotiate than more militant Indian groups. Rising civil disobedience and World War II eventually rendered India too costly and difficult to administer, and the British granted independence in 1947.

Independence: In some ways, the victory was bittersweet, as the country emerged with numerous political, social, and economic difficulties. On Independence Day (August 15, 1947), the country was partitioned into India and Pakistan, which led to massive migration of Hindus and Muslims and substantial communal conflict. Furthermore, the British had left India with a rudimentary industrial and scientific base; tremendous poverty; a large and growing population; social cleavages along caste and economic lines; and contentious territorial boundaries that have led to armed conflicts with Pakistan (1947 to 1949, 1965, 1971), China (1962), and numerous insurgent groups.

In spite of such difficulties, the nation can count a number of successes. With the exception of martial law from 1975 to 1977, India has maintained a democratic political system. Building on the British-established education system, India developed an educational infrastructure that has trained one of the world's largest scientific and technical populations. Using Green Revolution agricultural technologies, the country has become self-sufficient in food production. Moreover, a combination of socialist planning and free enterprise from the 1950s to the 1970s led to substantial industrialization with the goal of making India economically self-sufficient.

In the 1980s and 1990s, socialist economic planning and import substitution industries were slowly replaced by liberalization measures, a large middle class emerged, information technology developed into an important economic sector, and at times economic growth has been impressive. India has also become somewhat influential in international political and economic matters and appears set to continue those trends.

Numerous problems remain, however, such as substantial poverty, large income gaps between wealthy and poor, a large mass of people who lack the skills to participate in the new economy, and numerous insurgencies that threaten the nation's territorial integrity. Some social issues remain unresolved, and the rise of Hindu nationalism has become a particularly contentious topic in both Indian society and politics. Indeed, the Bharatiya Janata Party (BJP) led by Prime Minister Atal Bihari Vajpayee was in power from 1998 to 2004, and the BJP is often associated with Hindu nationalism. Furthermore, some observers believe the nation is facing difficulties in the political capacity to address these problems. Intense multiparty political competition over numerous economic and social issues has resulted in often-fragile coalitions of political parties, and no single political party has held a parliamentary majority since 1989. The government changed nine times from December 1989 to the elections in May 2004 in which the Indian National Congress returned to power under Prime Minister Manmohan Singh. Thus, increasing pluralism of political parties, growing diversity in interest-group representation, and substantial ideological divisions among parties are significant obstacles in policy implementation.

GEOGRAPHY

Location: India occupies much of the South Asian subcontinent, and the Indian mainland stretches eastward from Pakistan in the west to Bangladesh and Burma in the east. On the north, India borders China, Nepal, and Bhutan. The Indian Ocean to the south, the Arabian Sea to the west, and the Bay of Bengal to the east form the country's coastline. Noncontiguous to the mainland are the Lakshadweep Islands in the Arabian Sea and the Andaman and Nicobar Islands located 1,300 kilometers from the mainland in the Bay of Bengal.

Click to Enlarge Image

Size: The country's exact size is subject to debate because some borders are disputed. The Indian government lists the total area as 3,287,260 square kilometers and the total land area as 3,060,500 square kilometers; the United Nations lists the total area as 3,287,263 square kilometers and total land area as 2,973,190 square kilometers. In either case, India is the seventh largest country in the world and about one-third the size of the United States.

Land Boundaries: Land boundaries total 15,200 kilometers. India shares common borders with Pakistan (3,325 kilometers; the Jammu and Kashmir border is 1,085 kilometers), China (line of

4

actual control is 3,439 kilometers), Bhutan (605 kilometers), Nepal (1,690 kilometers), Burma (1,452 kilometers), and Bangladesh (4,339 kilometers). Although India and Sri Lanka do not share a land boundary, the narrowest distance between the two countries is only 64 kilometers across the Palk Strait.

Disputed Territory: Most of Jammu and Kashmir is contested with Pakistan, and the Aksai Chin area of Jammu and Kashmir is disputed with China, as is the border of Arunachal Pradesh state in northeast India. Nepal claims a 75-square-kilometer-area called Kalapani. Possession of recently emerged New Moore Island (South Talpatty) in the Bay of Bengal has been disputed by Bangladesh, and much of the border with Bangladesh is not demarcated.

Length of Coastline: India's total coastline is 7,516 kilometers in length, which comprises 5,422 kilometers for the mainland, 132 kilometers for the Lakshadweep Islands, and 1,962 kilometers for the Andaman and Nicobar Islands.

Maritime Claims: Under the 1982 United Nations Convention on the Law of the Sea, India has a 200-nautical-mile exclusive economic zone, a 12-nautical-mile territorial sea, a 24-nautical-mile contiguous zone, and a legal continental shelf extending to a depth of 2,500 meters or to the end of the continental margin.

Topography: There are three main geological regions: the Indo-Gangetic Plain and the Himalayas—collectively known as North India—and the Peninsula, or South India. These and other portions of India can be classified into diverse physiological regions that include highlands, plains, deserts, and river valleys. The country's lowest elevation is zero meters at the Indian Ocean, and the highest is 8,598 meters at Kanchenjunga, which is the third highest mountain in the world and located in the Himalayas.

Principal Rivers: India's longest rivers are the Brahmaputra and Indus, which are both 2,896 kilometers long, although neither is entirely within India. Other major rivers are the Ganga (Ganges, 2,525 kilometers), Godavari (1,465), Kaveri (Cauvery, 800), Krishna (1,401), Mahanandi (851), Narmada (1,312), and Yamuna (1,370).

Climate: Climate in India varies significantly from the permanently snow-capped Himalayas in the north to the tropics in the south. The country has four seasons. December to February is relatively dry and cool, March to May is dry and hot, from June to September predominating southwest maritime winds bring monsoon rains to most of the country, and in October and November there are retreating dry monsoons originating from the northeast. Average temperatures range from 12.5° C to 30° C in the northwest, 17.5° C to 30° C in the north and northeast, and 22.5° C to 30° C in the south. Average annual rainfall is around 1,000 to 1,500 millimeters for much of the country, but can be quite low in some parts of the northwest (150 to 300 millimeters annually) and very high in the northeast and along the west coast (1,500 to 2,500 millimeters annually).

Natural Resources: Commercially important natural resources include arable land, bauxite, chromite, coal (fourth-largest reserves in the world), diamonds, iron ore, limestone, manganese, mica, natural gas, petroleum, and titanium ore.

Land Use: In 2000 the total arable land and land planted under permanent crops combined was 1,697,000 square kilometers, and total irrigated land was 548,000 square kilometers. The total of non-arable land and land not under permanent crops was 1,276,190 square kilometers.

Environmental Factors: India is vulnerable to various natural hazards, particularly cyclones and annual monsoon floods, and various combinations of poverty, population growth, increasing individual consumption, industrialization, infrastructural development, poor agricultural practices, and resource maldistribution have led to substantial human transformation of India's natural environment. An estimated 60 percent of cultivated land suffers from soil erosion, waterlogging, and salinity. It is also estimated that between 4.7 and 12 billion tons of topsoil are lost annually from soil erosion. From 1947 to 2002, average annual per capita water availability declined by almost 70 percent to 1,822 cubic meters, and overexploitation of groundwater is problematic in the states of Haryana, Punjab, and Uttar Pradesh. Forest area covers 19.4 percent of India's geographic area (63.7 million hectares). Nearly half of the country's forest cover is found in the state of Madhya Pradesh (20.7 percent) and the seven states of the northeast (25.7 percent); the latter is experiencing net forest loss. Forest cover is declining because of harvesting for fuel wood and the expansion of agricultural land. These trends, combined with increasing industrial and motor vehicle pollution output, have led to atmospheric temperature increases, shifting precipitation patterns, and declining intervals of drought recurrence in many areas. The Indian Agricultural Research Institute has estimated that a 3° C rise in temperature will result in a 15 to 20 percent loss in annual wheat yields. These are substantial problems for a nation with such a large population depending on the productivity of primary resources and whose economic growth relies heavily on industrial growth.

Civil conflicts involving natural resources—most notably forests and arable land—have occurred in eastern and northeastern states. By contrast, water resources have not been linked to either domestic or international violent conflict as was previously anticipated by some observers. Possible exceptions include some communal violence related to distribution of water from the Kaveri River and political tensions surrounding actual and potential population displacements by dam projects, particularly on the Narmada River.

Time Zones: All of India is under a single time zone, which is Greenwich Mean Time plus 5.5 hours.

SOCIETY

Population: The 2004 estimate of India's total population was 1,065,070,607. According to the 2001 Indian census, the total population was 1,028,610,328, a 21.3 percent increase from 1991 and 2 percent average growth rate from 1975 to 2001. India has nearly 17 percent of the world's population, second only to China. About 72 percent of the population resided in rural areas in 2001, yet the country has a population density of 324 persons per square kilometer. Major states have more than 400 persons per square kilometer, but population densities are around 150 persons or fewer per square kilometer in some border states and insular territories.

Demography: In 2001 India's birthrate was 25.4 per 1,000 population, its death rate was 8.4 per 1,000, and its infant mortality rate was 66 per 1,000 live births. In 1995 to 1997, India's total fertility rate was 3.4 children per woman (4.5 in 1980–82). According to the 2001 Indian census, 35.3 percent of the population was under 14 years of age, 59.9 percent between 15 and 64, and 4.8 percent 65 and older (the 2004 estimates are, respectively, 31.7 percent, 63.5 percent, and 4.8 percent); the sex ratio was 933 females per 1,000 males. In 2004 India's median age was estimated to be 24.4. From 1992 to 1996, overall life expectancy at birth was 60.7 years (60.1 years for males and 61.4 years for females) and was estimated to be 64 years in 2004 (63.3 for males and 64.8 for females).

Ethnic Groups: The exact number of ethnic groups depends on source and method of counting, and scholars estimate that only the continent of Africa exceeds the linguistic, cultural, and genetic diversity of India. Seventy-two percent of the population is Indo-Aryan, 25 percent Dravidian, and 3 percent Mongoloid and other. Each of these groups can be further subdivided into various—and changing—combinations of language, religion, and, very often, caste. The Hindu caste system is technically illegal but widely practiced (generally more in rural areas) and comprises four major categories (*varnas*) that are found India-wide but are often subdivided into hundreds of sub-categories (*jatis*), many of which are often found only in specific areas. Similar hereditary and occupational social hierarchies exist within Sikh and Muslim communities but are generally far less pervasive and institutionalized. About 16 percent of the total population is "untouchable" (Scheduled Castes is the more formal, legal term; *Dalit* is the term preferred by "untouchables" and roughly translates to downtrodden); around 8 percent of the population belongs to one of 461 indigenous groups (often called Scheduled Tribes for legal purposes, although the term *adivasi* is commonly used).

Languages: The total number of languages and dialects varies by source and counting method, and many Indians speak more than one language. The Indian census lists 114 languages (22 of which are spoken by one million or more persons) that are further categorized into 216 dialects or "mother tongues" spoken by 10,000 or more speakers. An estimated 850 languages are in daily use, and the Indian Government claims there are more than 1,600 dialects.

Hindi is the official language and the most commonly spoken, but not all dialects are mutually comprehensible. English also has official status and is widely used in business and politics, although knowledge of English varies widely from fluency to knowledge of just a few words. The teaching of Hindi and English is compulsory in most states and union territories. Twenty-two languages are legally recognized by the constitution for various political, educational, and other purposes: Assamese, Bengali, Bodo, Dogri, Gujarati, Hindi, Kannada, Kashmiri, Konkani, Maithali, Malayalam, Manipuri, Marathi, Nepali, Oriya, Punjabi, Sanskrit, Santhali, Sindhi, Tamil, Telugu, and Urdu. Numerous other languages are recognized by individual states but not officially recognized by the central government, and linguistic issues related to education, employment, and politics are sometimes politically contentious. Indeed, some state borders are based on linguistic lines. The most commonly spoken languages are Hindi (40.2 percent of the population), Bengali (8.3 percent), Telugu (7.9 percent), Marathi (7.5 percent), and Tamil (6.3 percent).

Religion: Approximately 80.5 percent of the population is Hindu, 13.4 percent Muslim, 2.3 percent Christian, 1.9 percent Sikh, 0.8 percent Buddhist, and 0.4 percent Jain; another 0.6 percent belongs to other faiths, such as Zoroastrianism and numerous religions associated with Scheduled Tribes. These percentages have changed little since the 1961 census. In spite of Hinduism's inherent pantheism, adherents often focus much of their devotion on a specific deity—such as Vaishnivites (those primarily devoted to Vishnu and related deities) and Shaivites (Shiva and related deities)—but these denominations rarely have notable social, economic, or political consequences. The Indian constitution confers religious freedom for individuals and prohibits religious discrimination, but in spite of this, there have been enduring tensions—and occasional conflict—among religious communities, most notably between Hindus and Muslims.

Education and Literacy: In 2000 the adult literacy rate (percent aged 15 or older) was 58.5 percent (72.3 percent for males, 44.4 percent for females). These figures have all nearly doubled since 1961 and are higher than in most other South Asian nations, but they are still far lower than in most East Asian nations. In 2001 the combined primary, secondary, and tertiary enrollment ratio was 55 percent of the population of official school age for the three levels. Total government expenditures on education in 2001 were Rs841.8 billion (US$17.3 billion), which was 13.2 percent of all government expenditures and 4 percent of gross domestic product (GDP). Since the 1950s, government expenditures on education have increased steadily, as have the number of educational institutions from the primary to the university level.

In most states and union territories, primary school covers grade levels (called "standards") 1 to 8 and secondary education, standards 9 and 10; all states have senior secondary education for standards 11 and 12. As of 1997, most states and union territories had no compulsory level of education. Twelve states and union territories legally require completion of either the fifth- or eighth-grade level, yet drop-out rates are high even in compulsory stages. The majority of states and union territories have free education up to the seventh-grade level, and the majority of primary schools are government funded and managed. However, less than half of secondary schools are government funded and managed. Indeed, 34 percent of secondary institutions are government funded but privately managed, and 25 percent are privately managed without government funding.

Health: National health indicators are generally lower than in many developing countries but have shown dramatic improvement nationwide, although there are variations among states in India. India's 2002 Human Development Index (HDI is a measure of income, education, and health developed by the United Nations) of 0.595 was an improvement over its 1975 HDI of 0.411, but India ranked 127th in the world out of 177 countries (the 2002 world average HDI was 0.729). An estimated 21 percent of the total population is malnourished, and common diseases include malaria, filariasis, leprosy, cholera, pneumonic plague, tuberculosis, trachoma, goiter, and diarrheal diseases. According to government estimates, about 0.5 percent of the population (about 5.1 million) was infected by the human immunodeficiency virus (HIV) in 2003. In November 2004, the head of the United Nations Acquired Immune Deficiency Syndrome program (UNAIDS) claimed that India, along with China and Russia, is on the "tipping point" of having small, localized AIDS epidemics become major ones that could detrimentally affect the world's capacity to prevent and treat the disease.

The above facts and figures are associated with substantial poverty and relatively low government health expenditures. In 2001 public health expenditures were 3.1 percent of total general government expenditures but only 17.9 percent of total health expenditures. By contrast, private expenditures were 82.1 percent of total health expenditures, all of which was out-of-pocket expense. Furthermore, total health expenditures per capita represented 5.1 percent of gross domestic product (GDP) in 2001, but public health expenditures were only 0.9 percent of GDP, and private health expenditures were 4.2 percent of GDP. The population's health is also a function of the relatively low number of health personnel and low level of infrastructure, which are on a par with many countries in Sub-Saharan Africa. In 1991 public and private primary health centers included more than 14,000 hospitals, 28,000 dispensaries, and 838,000 beds. In 1998 there were 52.2 medical practitioners per 100,000 persons, and in 1994 there were 69 hospital beds per 100,000 persons. In 1992 India had 48 physicians and 45 nurses per 100,000 persons.

Welfare: Generally, central (union) government welfare expenditures are a substantial portion of the official budget, and state and local governments play important roles in developing and implementing welfare policies. In 2000 union government expenditures on social services (includes education, health, family welfare, women and child development, and social justice and empowerment), rural development, and basic minimum services were approximately US$7.7 billion (Rs361.7 billion), which was 11.1 percent of total government expenditures and 1.7 percent of gross domestic product (GDP). Furthermore, the union and state governments maintain a plethora of reserved seats in various political and education institutions for lower castes, indigenous persons, and others based on their percentage of the population. Finally, various innovative development programs have been developed—often at state or local levels—for social development and the empowerment of women and lower castes, and the state of Kerala is internationally known for its noteworthy success in public welfare.

ECONOMY

Overview: From 1947 to the late 1970s, the economy was characterized by central government planning and import substitution industries, and economic production was transformed from primarily agriculture, forestry, fishing, and textile manufacturing to various heavy industries, transportation, and telecommunications. Agriculture still employs nearly 60 percent of the population, but accounts for only 22.6 percent of gross domestic product (GDP). By the 1980s and 1990s, private-sector initiatives noticeably increased, and information technology emerged in importance but has proven vulnerable to changes in foreign demand, out-migration of information technology labor, and a weak but growing domestic market for information technology goods and services.

In the 1980s, government liberalization measures—such as privatization of government industries and reduced tariffs on imported capital goods—have been credited for 1990s economic growth rates of around 4 to 7 percent annually, nearly double the 3 percent growth rates that characterized the previous 40 years. Furthermore, foreign direct investment has increased to an annual range of US$3 billion to US$5 billion, but is seen as hampered by corruption and bureaucratic inefficiency and remains well behind foreign direct investment in neighboring

China. Furthermore, India accounts for less than 1 percent of world trade in spite of having 18 percent of the world's population, and the informal economy accounts for 23.1 percent of gross national income (the new term for gross national product). A new union government was elected in May 2004 and is under significant pressure to provide greater economic development in rural areas.

Gross Domestic Product (GDP)/Power Purchasing Parity (PPP): In 2002 GDP was US$496.8 billion (Rs24.2 trillion). Since the early 1990s, GDP has grown 4 to 7 percent annually, which is higher than GDP growth for the European Union, the United States, or the world as a whole. In 2003 PPP per capita was US$2,880.

Government Budget: Government revenues and expenditures have grown substantially since the early 1990s. According to India's Ministry of Finance, in 2002–03 tax and non-tax revenues were US$49.7 billion (Rs2.3 trillion), total expenditures were US$88.9 billion (Rs4.1 trillion), and the fiscal deficit was US$31.1 billion (Rs1.5 trillion). Government expenditures generally have been highest in the energy, transportation, and social service sectors, which receive about two-thirds of total government expenditures. Tax revenues have grown annually around 10 percent or more since the early 1950s, and tax receipts have increased even more substantially since the mid-1990s with accelerated economic growth and improved government revenue collection capacities. For example, total tax revenues were US$20.8 billion for 1994–95 and US$35.2 billion for 2002–03. Fiscal deficits, however, have also increased from US$17.8 billion in 1994–95 to an estimated US$31.1 billion for 2002–03.

Agriculture, Forestry, and Fishing: Since independence, India has changed from a food importer to a food exporter, but agriculture has declined as a percentage of gross domestic product (GDP; from 32.8 percent in 1991 to 22.6 percent in 2001) and total exports (from 18.5 percent to 14.2 percent). Around 46 percent (141 million hectares) of total land is cultivated, and 16 percent is double cropped (49 million hectares), effectively giving India 190 million hectares of cultivated land. Another 4.8 percent (14.7 million hectares) is permanent pastureland or planted in tree crops or groves. Agriculture continues to employ the major, but declining, proportion of workers (from 69.4 percent in 1951 to 58.4 percent in 2001) and agricultural employment varies substantially among states (from 38.9 percent of workers in Punjab to 77.3 percent in Bihar). Most farmers cultivate plots of two hectares or less, and large landholders have only been divested in a few areas. Agricultural output—and the food security of millions—remains susceptible to often-tenuous access to arable land, credit, fertilizers, and irrigation as well as to natural conditions, particularly annual variations in rainfall.

The remarkable growth in agricultural output is largely due to Green Revolution inputs such as high-yield seed varieties and fertilizers. Rice, wheat, pulses, and oilseeds dominate production, but millet, corn, and sorghum are also important crops. The main commercial crops are sugar (India is the world's second largest producer), rice (world's second largest exporter), wheat, cotton, and jute. However, the rate of output for several crops may have peaked, and problems with soil degradation, rural infrastructure, and declining per capita agricultural holdings may prevent the rate of agricultural growth from keeping pace with increasing rates of population growth and per capita food consumption.

In 1991, 2.1 percent of the population was employed in forestry, fishing, livestock, hunting, and related activities. As a percentage of GDP, forestry has declined from 1.5 percent in 1993–94 to 1.1 percent in 2000–01. In the same period, fishing changed little from 1.1 percent to 1.2 percent of GDP.

Mining and Minerals: Since the early 1990s, mining has accounted for around 2 to 3.5 percent of gross domestic product (GDP) and employed less than 1 percent of the labor force. The majority of minerals produced by India are bauxite, copper, iron, lead, mica, rare earths, uranium ore, and zinc.

Industry and Manufacturing: For decades, Indian industries were largely import substitution industries producing textiles, steel and aluminum, fertilizers and petrochemicals, and electronics and motor vehicles. From 1950 to 2000, industrial output increased from 15 to 27 percent of gross domestic product (GDP), but the sector continues to employ only about 10 percent of the workforce. Several industries face problems with power availability, high interest rates, customs delays, and regulatory obstacles. Domestic automobile manufacturing has increased substantially since the end of government licensing of automobile production in 1995, and car sales rose 50 percent by 2000. Import liberalization has also led to lowered sales for domestic industries, such as computer hardware and cement.

Energy: India is the world's sixth largest energy consumer, and the nation faces substantial challenges in meeting both present and expected demands for energy, particularly electric power. India has a growing nuclear power industry and abundant hydroelectric power (particularly in North India), and it is the world's third largest producer of coal (which provides more than half of domestic energy needs). But it is also a growing consumer and importer of petroleum and natural gas, and consumption of these products is expected to increase substantially. The government appears to be addressing petroleum demand by limiting imports and by expanding domestic exploration and production, but several factors provide little optimism that such measures will be sufficient for future demands. The government continues to pursue various reforms in the electricity sector, but it has abandoned full privatization of the state-owned petroleum industry, raising questions about its commitment to reforms in the petroleum sector. Finally, India faces economic competition from China over potential oil and gas resources in the Indian Ocean that both countries need for their economic development.

Services: From 1951 to 2000, business, information technology, banking, communications, hotels, and other services increased from 27 to 48 percent of gross domestic product (GDP), but most of this growth occurred in the 1990s. The percentage of the Indian workforce employed in services was 23.5 percent in 2000. Information technology services have emerged as an important element of the economy, but the information technology sector is believed to be vulnerable to out-migration of information technology professionals, particularly when the global economy is strong.

Banking and Finance: Under 1990s liberalization measures, restrictions on foreign direct investment have been relaxed, and foreign banks have been allowed to have greater shareholding in domestic banks (up to 49 percent), although foreign banks have faced some difficulties in acquiring such stakes. In 2002 government legislation enhanced banks' capacity to act against debtors, a measure that should help banks in their attempts to address the high level of bad debt held by Indian companies.

Tourism: Tourism industry analysts estimate that India is one of the world's fastest growing tourism markets with an annual growth rate of approximately 8.8 percent. Annual tourist inflows range between 2 and 2.5 million, but tourism has proven to be susceptible to issues such as communal conflict between Hindus and Muslims and occasional spikes in tensions between India and Pakistan.

Labor: The total number of persons in the labor force is unknown. According to official figures, from 1981 to 2001 the total number of workers grew more than 50 percent from approximately 245 million to 402 million persons. These figures count only those who are considered to have "engaged in economically productive activity for 183 days or more." The actual number of persons in the labor force is likely to be much higher. From 1983 to 1994, the nation's unemployment rate declined from 8.3 percent to 6 percent and then increased to 7.3 percent by 2000. Unemployment rates have historically been higher in urban areas, but rural and urban unemployment rates became nearly equal by 2000 (7.2 and 7.7 percent, respectively).

Foreign Economic Relations: India's principal export and import trades are with the European Union, the United States, and Japan. Most aid is provided by the Aid-to-India Consortium, consisting of the World Bank Group, Austria, Belgium, Britain, Canada, Denmark, France, Germany, Italy, Japan, the Netherlands, Norway, Sweden, and the United States. Japan is the largest aid granter and lender. India has its own aid programs with Bangladesh, Bhutan, Nepal, and Vietnam.

Imports: Principal imports are petroleum and petroleum products, capital goods, uncut gems, machinery, and fertilizer. Major imports are from the United States, the European Union (particularly Belgium), Singapore, the United Kingdom, and Saudi Arabia. In 2003 imports totaled US$64.5 billion, a substantial increase over 2002 imports of US$54.2 billion.

Exports: Principal exports are textile goods, finished gems and jewelry, engineered goods (including iron and steel), chemicals, and leather and leather goods. Main destinations of exports are the United States, the United Kingdom, China (particularly Hong Kong), Japan, and the European Union (particularly Germany). In 2003 total exports were valued at US$52.5 billion, a substantial increase over 2002 exports of US$47.7 billion.

Trade Balance: India's negative trade balance has grown steadily since the late 1980s. In 2003 exports were US$52.5 billion and imports were US$65.4 billion, resulting in a negative trade balance of US$12.9 billion.

Balance of Payments: Before 2002 India's surpluses in the capital account were offset by deficits in the current account, but since 2002 India has had surpluses in the current and capital accounts, leading to an accumulation of foreign reserves. The current account surplus is a small percentage of gross domestic product (0.5 percent in 2003) and has been the result of non-factor services and private transfers exceeding trade deficits. Growth in foreign direct investment is largely responsible for steady growth in the capital account, and external commercial borrowings and assistance make up most net outflows.

External Debt: India's total external debt has increased from US$83.8 billion in 1991 to US$112.1 billion in 2003, but external debt declined as a percentage of gross domestic product (GDP) in the same time period (from 28.7 to 20.2 percent). Furthermore, in 1991 India was the world's third highest debtor nation, but it had dropped to eighth by 2002.

Foreign Investment: Foreign direct investment in India has increased from about US$97 million in 1991 to US$3.6 billion for 2003, partly because of various liberalization measures, such as reduced tariffs and relaxed restrictions on foreign ownership of domestic industries.

Currency and Exchange Rate: The rupee (Rs) has depreciated steadily against the dollar since the 1970s. The average annual exchange rate for 2003 was US$1=Rs46.59 and US$1=Rs31.29 for 1993. In December 2004, the exchange rate was approximately US$1=Rs44. Since the late 1990s, the rupee has been stable against the euro as a result of the weakening of the U.S. dollar and worldwide shift away from U.S. dollar assets.

Fiscal Year: India's fiscal year runs from April 1 to March 31.

TRANSPORTATION AND TELECOMMUNICATIONS

Overview: India's transportation infrastructure has undergone tremendous change since independence. While traditional, non-mechanized transport means are still quite common (elephants and camels are not an uncommon sight even in large urban areas), roads, railroads, ports, and aviation continue to expand. India now has the world's second largest road network, and its rail network is among the most used in the world for passengers and freight. Furthermore, increasing incomes and government liberalization measures have contributed to tremendous growth in the numbers of automobiles, two- and three-wheeled vehicles, private and public buses, and urban rail networks. However, there are significant, accompanying problems with pollution, increasing traffic density, unauthorized transportation providers, and high numbers of traffic fatalities.

Roads: There were about 3.3 million kilometers of roads by 2002, of which 1.4 million kilometers were surfaced and more than 1 million kilometers were covered with gravel, crushed stone, or earth. More than 150 highways are rated as national highways and carry about 40 percent of road traffic on a total length of 65,569 kilometers. Around 85 percent of all passenger traffic and 70 percent of all freight traffic travel by road. By 2007, highways are expected to expand by 13,146 kilometers, with road projects aimed at linking the country's major cities and spanning the entire country north-south and east-west. Modes of road transport are a mix of traditional and modern means. Urban transit is dominated by motor vehicles, with increasing use of automobiles, minibuses, buses, trucks, and particularly two- and three-wheeled vehicles. However, bullocks, camels, elephants, and other beasts of burden are seen on Indian roads, even in urban areas.

Railroads: All railroads are government-owned and operated by Indian Railways. In 2002 total route length was 63,028 kilometers, and double and multiple tracks resulted in a total track length of 108,706 kilometers. Of the total track length, 86,526 kilometers were 1.676-millimeter gauge, 18,529 kilometers were 1.000-millimeter gauge, and 3,651 kilometers were 0.762- and 0.610-millimeter gauge. About 16,000 kilometers were electrified, mostly 1.676 millimeter gauge. The rail system includes 7,566 locomotives, 37,840 coaches, 222,147 freight wagons, 6,853 stations, and nearly 116,000 bridges. Both passenger and freight carriage continue to expand annually, and the rail system is the fourth most heavily used in the world, both for passengers and freight. For the financial year 2004, Indian Railways carried 557 million freight tons and more than 5 billion passengers. There are some high-speed routes and increasing use of them. Most rolling stock and other components are still domestically produced, but they are increasingly manufactured through commercial agreements with foreign companies. There have been major government investments in modernization since the early 1990s, but Indian Railways has also experienced dwindling government budgetary support and has suffered from the dual role of being both a public utility and a commercial enterprise.

India also has several urban passenger rail systems. Kolkata (Calcutta) has a full metro system, and New Delhi's metro system is operational and expanding. Chennai has a rapid transit system, and there are suburban rail networks in Bangalore, Mumbai (Bombay), and New Delhi. There are plans for metro, light rail, or both in Bangalore, Coimbatore, Hyderabad, Jaipur, Lucknow, Mumbai, and Pune.

Ports: India has 12 major ports and 185 minor and intermediate ports along the country's coastline. There are also 7 shipyards under the control of the central government, 2 shipyards controlled by state governments, and 19 privately owned shipyards. The major ports handled 344.6 million tons of cargo for the financial year 2004, with Chennai, Kandla, and Vishakhapatnam carrying the greatest tonnage. Major ports can collectively handle 390 million tons of cargo annually, and port operations have improved since the mid-1990s. All major ports, except one (Ennore), are government administered, but private-sector participation in ports has increased. In 2000 there were 102 shipping companies operating in India, of which five were privately owned and based in India and one was owned by the government (Shipping Corporation of India). In 2000 there were 639 government-owned ships, including 91 oil tankers, 79 dry cargo bulk carriers, and 10 cellular container vessels. Indian-flagged vessels carried about 15 percent of overseas cargo at Indian ports for financial year 2003.

Inland and Coastal Waterways: According to official sources, India has approximately 14,500 kilometers of inland waterways, but the transportation potential is vastly underused. More than 3,600 kilometers are navigable by large vessels, although only about 2,000 kilometers are used. For purposes of navigational development and conservation, three inland waterways have been declared national waterways: the Allahabad-Haldia portion of the Ganga-Bhagirathi-Hooghly rivers (1,620 kilometers), the Sadiya-Dhubri section of the Brahmaputra River (891 kilometers), and a combination of western canals (205 kilometers).

Civil Aviation and Airports: The government owns two airlines (Air India and Indian Airlines) and one helicopter service (Pawan Hans), and there are twelve privately owned airlines. Private airlines account for about 45 percent of domestic air traffic, and as of 2003 the government had divested more than 50 percent of the equity in both government-owned airlines. Of 288 airports, 208 have permanent-surface runways, and there are two runways of more than 3,659 meters. The Airports Authority of India administers 126 airports: 11 international, 89 domestic, and 26 for defense purposes. In 2003 these airports collectively handled approximately 500,000 flights, 40 million passengers, and 900,000 tons of cargo. Major international airports are located in Kolkata (Calcutta), Madras (Chennai), Mumbai (Bombay), New Delhi, and Thiruvananthapuram (Trivandrum). There is also international service from Bangalore, Guwahati, Hyderabad, and Mamargao, and there are major regional airports at Ahmadabad, Allahabad, Chandigarh, Kochi (Cochin), Nagpur, Pune, Srinagar, and Thiruvananthapuram.

Pipelines: In 2003 India had an estimated 5,798 kilometers of gas pipelines, 1,195 kilometers for liquid petroleum gas, 5,613 kilometers for oil, and 5,567 kilometers for refined products. India and Iran have discussed constructing a gas pipeline, but the Indian government and oil industry analysts have expressed concerns about the pipeline's security because of its proposed route through conflict-prone areas of Pakistan.

Telecommunications: India is witnessing possibly its greatest period of change in communications, with increasing shifts from government to private providers and greater public use of various technologies. From 1995 to 2003, the number of Internet users increased from 250,000 to 18.4 million. Since the late 1990s, the number of telephones, mobile phones, and personal computers has increased substantially. In 2004 there were 40.9 million telephones and 26.2 million mobile phones, and in 2003 there were an estimated 7.5 million personal computers. Some basic telephone services were opened to private-sector competition in 1994, and portions of state-owned telecommunications services have been purchased by private entities. Government-owned radio (All India Radio) and television (Doordarshan) networks have extensive national and local coverage, but domestic and international private television networks are increasingly prolific through cable and satellite. According to government figures, there were 79.4 million television households in 2001. From 1991 to 2002, the number of radios roughly doubled to an estimated 111 million, and radio remains the main source of news for most Indians.

GOVERNMENT AND POLITICS

Government Overview: India is a democratic republic with a system of government legally based on the often-amended 1950 constitution. The central government is also known as the union government, and its structure is much like the British parliamentary system, with distinct, but interrelated executive, legislative, and judicial branches. State governments are structured much like the central government, and district governments exist in a variety of forms. The Indian parliament is a bicameral legislature composed of a lower house (the Lok Sabha or House of the People), with 543 popularly elected members and 2 members appointed by the president, and an upper house (the Rajya Sabha or Council of States), with 12 appointed members and 233 members elected by state and union territory assemblies. Lok Sabha members serve five-year terms, and Rajya Sabha members serve six-year terms, with one-third of members up for election every two years. The legislature passes laws on constitutionally specified matters, such as central government finances and constitutional amendments. The two houses have the same powers, but the Rajya Sabha's power in the legislative process is subordinate to the Lok Sabha.

India has both a prime minister and a president. Members of parliament and state legislative assemblies elect the president, currently A.P.J. Abdul Kalam, who was elected in 2002. Prime ministers are leaders of the majority party in parliament but are formally appointed by the president. In 2004 Manmohan Singh became prime minister when his Indian National Congress party defeated the Bharatiya Janata Party led by Singh's predecessor as prime minister, Atal Bihari Vajpayee. Over time, political power has become increasingly concentrated in the prime minister and Council of Ministers (cabinet), although they are responsible to the parliament. The president's duties are mostly ceremonial, although the president formally approves the prime minister and also approves the Council of Ministers based on the prime minister's advice. Furthermore, all bills require presidential approval before becoming law. The vice president is ex officio chairperson of the Rajya Sabha and acts in place of the president when the president is unable to perform his or her duties.

The Supreme Court is the top legal entity, and it is composed of a chief justice appointed by the president and 25 associate judges also appointed by the president in consultation with the chief justice. The Supreme Court has numerous legal powers, such as appellate jurisdiction over all civil and criminal proceedings, with the potential of influencing interpretation of the constitution. The parliament and Supreme Court have maintained a contentious relationship on issues related to judicial review and parliamentary sovereignty. Below the Supreme Court are high courts, followed by a hierarchy of subordinate courts, and some states also have *panchayat* (village-level) courts that decide civil and criminal matters. Some high courts serve more than one state, and all are independent of state legislatures and executives. The judiciary is regarded as slow and cumbersome but is also widely respected and often takes an activist role in protecting citizens' rights.

Since independence, India has experienced a plethora of political successes and problems. Corruption, communal conflicts, and rural economic development remain difficult political issues. Furthermore, some analysts believe the government's inclusive design could undermine governing capacity and national unity as political parties and social groups press for their respective parochial interests. Yet the country maintains a democratic system of government with civil liberties that are often lacking in many poor, ethnically diverse societies. India also has an impressive record of economic development and a demonstrable commitment to correcting traditional social oppression. A wide variety of social groups have held elected office, and women, Sikhs, Muslims, and *dalits* have served as either president or prime minister. In 2004 there were 45 women elected to the Lok Sabha, and both *dalits* and indigenous groups have a certain minimum number of reserved seats in the Lok Sabha and state assemblies based on their respective percentages of the population.

Administrative Divisions: There are twenty-eight states and seven union territories including the national capital territory of New Delhi. State boundaries are often based on language or other social characteristics, and union territories tend to be geographically smaller and less populous than states. States and union territories contain 601 districts that are further subdivided into townships containing from 200 to 600 villages. The union government exercises greater control over union territories than over states, but the division of power between the union and state governments can appear blurred and even chaotic at times. Relationships between some state governments and the union government have been contentious, particularly when state governments are run by political parties that oppose the governing party or coalition in parliament. The tremendous variations in economic and social development among states suggest that state governments can have a greater influence on their populations than the union government. However, the union government still exercises considerable influence on states through numerous financial resources and its authority to assume control of states during times of emergency (called President's Rule), which the union government has done nearly 100 times since 1947.

Provincial and Local Government: Union territories have a council of ministers, a legislature, and a high court, but they are largely governed by the central or union government through a lieutenant governor or chief commissioner appointed by the prime minister. The structure of state governments largely mirrors that of the union government, with each state having a legislative assembly, chief minister, and high court. State government policies are largely implemented through state-level agencies, but union government agencies are also prevalent at local levels. District and local governments are generally weak, although some states have attempted to establish traditional village councils (*panchayats*) to address local matters.

State legislatures are usually unicameral with a legislative assembly composed of members elected for five-year terms. Bicameral state legislatures also have a legislative council that is largely advisory in its capacities, with members directly elected, indirectly elected, or nominated. States' chief ministers are the leaders of majority parties in state legislatures, and just as the prime minister is accountable to parliament, chief ministers are answerable to state legislatures. However, the popularity and party support of some chief ministers enable them to have some autonomy from their state legislature and a degree of influence that rivals that of the union government. States also have governors that are appointed by the president and accountable to the dominant political party in parliament. Although the position is largely honorific, governors do have important powers such as formal approval of chief ministers and their cabinets as well as the authority to recommend that the union government take control of a state government during times of emergency (President's Rule).

Judicial and Legal System: The legal system is derived from English common law and based on the 1950 constitution. Judges decide cases, and there is no trial by jury. Defendants can choose counsel independent of the government, and the government provides free legal counsel for defendants unable to afford such. The judiciary enforces the right to fair trial, and there are effective channels for appeal, but the judicial system is so overburdened with a case backlog that some courts barely function. In non-criminal matters, the government does not interfere with the personal status laws of Muslims and other communities on matters dealing with family law, inheritance, divorce, and discrimination against women.

The Indian constitution contains civil liberties called Fundamental Rights that are guaranteed to all citizens and include equality before the law and freedoms of speech, expression, religion, and association. Freedom of the press is not explicitly stated but is widely interpreted as included in the freedoms of speech and expression. The Fundamental Rights were also created with the objective of addressing historical social injustices and legally prohibit bonded labor, human trafficking, and discrimination based on religion, sex, race, caste, and birthplace. Still, the government has the authority to limit civil liberties in order to preserve public order, protect national security, and for other reasons.

Electoral System: The Election Commission is the independent government body that supervises parliamentary and state elections, which are massive and sometimes marred by violence. Elections for state assemblies and the Lok Sabha are held every five years unless called earlier, such as through a no-confidence vote of the government by the Lok Sabha. Indeed, elections are often held before the five-year limits because governments have often had difficulty staying in power for the full five-year term. In the 2004 general elections, there were more than 687,000 polling stations and 671.5 million voters. Since 1952, there have been 14 general elections, with voter turnout ranging from 55 to 64 percent of eligible voters. The legal voting age is 18. National and state legislative elections are similar to the British House of Commons and United States House of Representatives, in which members gain office by winning a plurality of votes in their local constituency. There are 543 parliamentary constituencies. The number of constituencies for state legislatures ranges from 32 to 403, with a total of 4,120 state constituencies nationwide.

Politics and Political Parties: From independence (1947) until 1989, the left-of-center Indian National Congress and its factions dominated national politics. In the 1990s, the center-right Bharatiya Janata Party (BJP) and the centrist Janata Dal emerged as influential political parties, although Congress returned to power in May 2004 with Manmohan Singh as prime minister. There are numerous national and state parties. Among the best known and most prominent are: Akali Dal, All-India Anna DMK (AIADMK), Asom Gana Parishad, Bahujan Samaj Party (BSP), Bharatiya Janata Party (BJP), Communist Party of India (CPI), Communist Party of India-Marxist (CPI-M), Dravida Munnetra Kazhagam (DMK), Indian National Congress, Rashtriya Janata Dal (RJD), Samajwadi Party, Samata Party, Shiv Sena, and Telugu Desam.

Since the late 1960s, minority parties in Parliament have often been majority parties in state legislatures. Since 1989, single political parties have generally failed to win a parliamentary majority. As a result, parliament is often run by coalitions of political parties. It is believed that the emergence of multiparty governments is caused by voters' frustration with political corruption and the fragmentation of electorate support among the growing number of political parties that represent specific parochial or local interests. Thus, those parties have strong support only in particular states. Furthermore, lower castes and other social groups have become more involved in politics as both voters and politicians. It remains to be seen if these trends are indicative of increasing social fragmentation as parties attempt to advance parochial interests or simply the result of a socially diverse population's increasing participation in politics.

Mass Media: India has more newspapers than any other nation, and newspaper readership annually grows by millions. There are a few state-run newspapers, but most print media are privately owned. There are more than 5,600 daily newspapers and more than 46,000 non-daily newspapers and print periodicals. In 2002 the government allowed print media to be up to 26 percent foreign owned, but the most powerful publishers are joint stock companies that frequently have other commercial and industrial holdings. Government authorities control most television channels, yet the growth of private FM and television stations has marked a shift away from mostly state-run electronic media such as Doordarshan (television) and All India Radio. Foreign television channels are available through cable television or Indian broadcasters. An estimated 42.3 percent of Indian households have a television, and 52.2 percent of those have cable or satellite transmission. Similarly, the number of Internet users has rapidly to an estimated 18.4 million users in 2003. Article 19 of India's constitution ensures freedom of speech and expression, but Article 19 also allows the government to place "reasonable restrictions" on the exercise of those rights under various circumstances, such as maintenance of public order, state security, and public morality. India does have a high degree of press and speech freedom, and the nation is not generally regarded as a major violator of civil liberties by international human rights organizations. However, the government and police have been accused of violating journalists' civil liberties.

Foreign Relations: India's Ministry of External Affairs is the governmental body that is officially responsible for making and implementing foreign policy, although India's prime ministers have often exercised substantial influence in foreign policy decision making. India's parliament and armed forces historically have had very limited roles in the formulation of foreign policy.

India's relations with all major nations traditionally have been based on principles of nonalignment and India's own economic development. The overlapping domestic and external dimensions of India's economic development continue to illustrate that many matters related to India's ongoing formation as a nation have international security implications. Attempts to promote economic growth have pushed India from its previous emphasis on domestic self-sufficiency to a major promoter of free trade and economic liberalization. Nonalignment, however, has been seriously tested as a viable basis for foreign policy with the erosion of U.S. and Soviet tensions and with India's interest in playing an influential role in regional and world politics. The demise of India's long-term ally the Soviet Union cost India precious military and financial aid as well as international leverage. Some analysts argue that India's demonstration of nuclear capabilities in 1998 was driven as much by domestic desires to protect Indian influence and prestige internationally as by regional security concerns. Post-Cold War shifts in military power and concerns with terrorism have led India to create stronger bilateral relations with China, Israel, the United States, and other nations.

The Ministry of External Affairs has generally been most concerned with relations with neighboring Nepal, Sri Lanka, and particularly Pakistan on issues concerning unresolved borders, natural resource distribution, immigration, and insurgent activity. India has often tried to use treaties, alliances, and economic coercion to counter actions by neighbors that India regards as security threats, although China and Pakistan have generally thwarted such attempts. Indeed, India's security concerns have been most pronounced with Pakistan, as exemplified by the two countries' newfound nuclear rivalry, the 1999 Kargil War in Jammu and Kashmir, and the 2001 terrorist attack on India's parliament, which Pakistan is suspected of supporting. In spite of these difficulties, tensions between India and Pakistan have periodically thawed, and in late 2004 the two countries demonstrated surprising public interest in resolving their enduring dispute over Jammu and Kashmir.

Membership in International Organizations: India is a member of numerous international organizations including: African Development Bank, Asian Development Bank, Association of Southeast Asian Nations (dialogue partner), Bank for International Settlements, Colombo Plan, Commonwealth, Food and Agriculture Organization of the United Nations, Group of Six, Group of 15, Group of 24, Group of 77, International Atomic Energy Agency, International Bank for Reconstruction and Development, International Chamber of Commerce, International Civil Aviation Organization, International Confederation of Free Trade Unions, International Development Association, International Federation of Red Cross and Red Crescent Societies, International Finance Corporation, International Fund for Agricultural Development, International Hydrographic Organization, International Labour Organization, International Maritime Organization, International Monetary Fund, International Olympic Committee, International Organization for Migration (observer), International Organization for Standardization, International Red Cross and Red Crescent Movement, International Telecommunication Union, Interpol, Nonaligned Movement, Organisation for the Prohibition of Chemical Weapons, Organization of American States (observer), Permanent Court of Arbitration, South Asian Association for Regional Cooperation, United Nations, United Nations Conference on Trade and Development, United Nations Educational, Scientific and Cultural Organization, United Nations High Commissioner for Refugees, United Nations Industrial Development Organization, United Nations Monitoring, Verification and Inspection Commission, Universal Postal Union, World Confederation of Labor, World Customs Organization, World Federation of Trade Unions, World Health Organization, World Intellectual Property Organization, World Meteorological Organization, World Tourism Organization, and World Trade Organization.

Major International Treaties: India is a signatory to numerous international treaties including: the Antarctic Treaty, Basel Convention on the Control of Transboundary Movements of Hazardous Substances, Biological and Toxin Weapons Convention, Chemical Weapons Convention, Conference on Disarmament, Convention on Biological Diversity, Convention on International Trade in Endangered Species of Wild Flora and Fauna, Convention on Migratory Species, Convention on the Physical Protection of Nuclear Material, Convention on the Prohibition of Military or Any Other Hostile Use of Environmental Modification Techniques, Convention on Wetlands of International Importance Especially as Waterfowl Habitat, Geneva Protocol, International Atomic Energy Association Safeguards Agreement, International Convention for the Regulation of Whaling, International Plant Protection Convention, International Tropical Timber Agreement 1983, International Tropical Timber Agreement 1994, Kyoto Protocol to the United Nations Framework Convention on Climate Change, Montreal Protocol on Substances that Deplete the Ozone layer, Nuclear Safety Convention, Partial Test Ban Treaty, Protocol of 1978 Relating to the International Convention for the Prevention of Pollution from Ships, Protocol on Environmental Protection to the Antarctic Treaty, United Nations Convention on the Law of the Sea, United Nations Convention to Combat Desertification, United Nations Framework Convention on Climate Change, and Vienna Convention for the Protection of the Ozone Layer. India is not a party to the Treaty on the Non-Proliferation of Nuclear Weapons (NPT) or the Missile Technology Control Regime. Indian governments have argued that the NPT does not reduce nuclear weapons proliferation by states already possessing nuclear weapons and that the NPT denies non-nuclear states the right to have nuclear weapons.

NATIONAL SECURITY

Armed Forces Overview: The prime minister and Council of Ministers formulate national security policy. Below this level is the civilian bureaucracy, which exercises important influence, primarily through the Defence Minister's Committee of the cabinet. The third tier of defense policy making is the Chiefs of Staffs Committee. These three levels are supported by intelligence organizations, scientific and technical advisory committees, defense production, and research and development groups. There are three military services—army, navy, and air force—and a number of paramilitary and reserve forces. The army has been the dominant service in terms of both percentage of budget allotted to the armed forces and percentage of persons serving in the armed forces.

The military has undergone tremendous change since the early 1990s, and the government and military have seriously appraised the military's capabilities and organization. India's great-power aspirations have been continually hindered by its capabilities, but the situation has changed with India's emergence as a nuclear power after successful nuclear tests in May 1998 (India has since pledged a unilateral moratorium on nuclear testing). The armed services' goals of force modernization (particularly the navy and air force) through new arms acquisitions and a "Revolution in Military Affairs" via information technology are constrained by budgetary, bureaucratic, personnel, and technological obstacles. Although the military has long desired to rely on domestically produced military goods, much matériel is imported. Indeed, the Defense Research and Development Organization (DRDO), the arm of the Department of Defence responsible for providing military hardware, has been criticized by both parliament and the military for failing to provide even basic equipment, and several DRDO projects have been behind schedule. The 1984 merger of the Department of Defence Production and the Department of Defence Supplies has not yet led to reliance on domestic production of military hardware.

Service chiefs and military officers continually suggest that the military should have greater input into defense policymaking and national security, and generally such a role is not viewed as a threat to civilian control of the military. Since 2001, the government has established the Defence Intelligence Agency (DIA), the Defence Acquisitions Council (DAC, which now controls the DRDO), and the National Security Council (NSC), which suggests that India has rethought its defense policymaking structure. The government has also proposed creating a Chief of Defence Staff. However, these changes have yet to make a major impact. Indeed, the NSC issued the draft nuclear doctrine but has not otherwise played an important role in defense policymaking and is criticized as an ad hoc organization.

In 2004 there were approximately 1,325,000 active-duty personnel, with 1,100,000 in the army, 55,000 in the navy (5,000 in naval aviation and 1,200 marines), and 170,000 in the air force. Reserve forces personnel totaled 535,000, and there were fourteen paramilitary forces (including the coast guard) under the control of various ministries with a total strength of 1,089,700 in 2004.

Foreign Military Relations: India's most important bilateral relationship was with the Soviet Union, whose breakup cost India both a consistent soft-currency supplier of arms and a guardian of its interests in international forums. Since the late 1990s, arms purchases from Russia have increased, and military relations between the countries have changed from a buyer-seller relationship to collaborative development of military systems and occasional joint military exercises. Furthermore, in 2000 India and Russia signed a Declaration of Strategic Relationship that addresses military and technical cooperation and "deepening service to service cooperation." India has strengthened bilateral defense links with France, Israel, Poland, South Africa, and the United States through various combinations of military acquisitions, agreements, and joint exercises. India has also attempted to project its influence beyond South Asia by engaging in occasional joint operations with Indian Ocean nations and participating in its first summit with the Association of Southeast Asian Nations in November 2002.

Furthermore, Indian peacekeeping forces have been sent to Sri Lanka from 1987 to 1990 and to the Maldives in 1988. Since 1950 Indian military and police contingents have participated in United Nations (UN) peacekeeping forces in Angola, Bosnia and Herzegovina, Cambodia, Democratic Republic of the Congo, Costa Rica, Cyprus, Dominican Republic, El Salvador, Ethiopia and Eritrea, Gaza, Guatemala, Honduras, Iraq, Korea (during the Korean War), Kuwait, Laos, Lebanon, Liberia, Mozambique, Namibia, Nicaragua, Rwanda, Sierra Leone, Somalia, Vietnam, West New Guinea (West Irian), Yemen, and Yugoslavia. India has also provided police personnel and monitors for UN peacekeeping operations in Angola, Bosnia and Herzegovina, Cambodia, Haiti, Kosovo, Mozambique, Sierra Leone, and Western Sahara.

Foreign Military Forces: The only foreign military forces in India are with the United Nations Military Observer Group in India and Pakistan (UNMOGIP), which has 45 military observers from 9 countries stationed in Jammu and Kashmir.

External Threat: External security threats come from neighboring countries and insurgents using foreign border areas as havens for activities in India. Countries such as Bangladesh, Bhutan, and Sri Lanka present no conventional military threat to India, but their inability to police and control areas bordering India has provided Indian insurgents with havens. Indian government and military officials have publicly expressed concern about the political instability in Nepal posed by the Maoist insurgents. As far as external threats posed by other countries, popular opinion tends to regard Pakistan as the principal enemy, largely because of the Kashmir conflict and Pakistan's suspected links to numerous South Asian militant groups. However, the defense establishment generally regards China as the chief external threat, because of perceived Chinese attempts to isolate India militarily and diplomatically from the rest of Asia and perceived Chinese efforts to prevent India from becoming a permanent member of the United Nations (UN) Security Council. While China-India border issues remain unresolved from the Indian point of view, Sino-Indian relations have improved as China has adopted a less intimate relationship with Pakistan.

Defense Budget: India's defense budget has grown tremendously since the early 1990s, and India accounts for more than two-thirds of South Asian military spending. India's defense budget was approximately US$16.6 billion in 2003, about 2.5 percent of gross domestic product (GDP), and the 2004 defense budget is US$19.1 billion. By contrast, the 1994 defense budget was

US$7.6 billion, which was also 2.5 percent of GDP in 1994. Interestingly, as a result of inefficient equipment procurement processes, defense expenditures are often less than the defense budget (around 5 percent less).

Major Military Units: The army has an estimated 800,000 active-duty troops and 300,000 reserves. The army is structured as 12 corps, 4 field armies, and 3 armored divisions under central control and organized into 5 regional commands. The Northern regional command consists of three corps with eight infantry and five mountain divisions; the Western regional command has one armored, five infantry, and three "RAPID" divisions; the Central regional command has one corps with one armored, one infantry, and one RAPID division; the Eastern regional command has three corps with one infantry and seven mountain divisions; and the Southern regional command has two corps with one armored and three infantry divisions. The navy has an estimated 55,000 persons on active duty and an equal number of reserve troops. Navy units are structured into three area commands, and there are six naval bases with three more under construction. The air force has an estimated 170,000 active forces and 140,000 reserves. Air force units are under five regional air commands.

Major Military Equipment: The army's main equipment includes an estimated 3,898 main battle tanks, 1,600 armored infantry fighting vehicles, 317 armored personnel carriers, 4,175 towed artillery, 200 self-propelled artillery, 150 multiple rocket launchers, 2,424 air defense guns, and 100 helicopters. The navy's arsenal is composed of 1 aircraft carrier, 18 submarines, 8 destroyers, 16 frigates, 26 corvettes, 7 amphibious ships, 88 fixed-wing aircraft, and more than 100 helicopters. The air force's principal equipment consists of 679 combat aircraft of various types and 40 armed helicopters. India and its perennial rival, Pakistan, have developed nuclear weapons, ostensibly to deter foreign hostility, yet periodic fighting in Kashmir—such as the 1999 Kargil War—suggests that the theoretical logic of deterrence has not yet taken hold.

For decades, the military has aspired to domestic production of most items, but it relies heavily on imports of both simple items, such as clothing, and complex weapons systems. Observers contend that India has not done well with the production of tanks, helicopters, and submarines, but has fared better with missiles, small arms, and naval craft. Moreover, India's substantial spending on defense has stirred some debate about how much the defense industry should be privatized in order to avoid a collapse similar to that suffered by the Soviet Union. However, it is believed that the Ministry of Defence's civilian bureaucracy opposes privatization in order to protect employment in an overstaffed state bureaucracy. There has been some consideration of exporting arms to make up for budget shortfalls, but exports—and concrete efforts to increase them—remain minimal.

Military Service: The minimum age of service is 16, and the mandatory age for retirement for officers varies from 48 to 60 depending on rank. The military has expressed concern about its increasing age profile and a shortage of officers. Formal military service is completely on a volunteer basis, and India does not have—and never has had—conscription. However, a 2004 public opinion poll suggests that the Indian public is in favor of conscription.

Paramilitary Forces: Police are under the control of state governments, and the central government can assist states by providing central paramilitary forces as deemed necessary, particularly to guard coasts, borders, and sensitive military areas and to aid local police forces against insurgencies. There is also a great deal of interest in improving paramilitary training, hardware, and domestic intelligence, as paramilitary forces are often outdone by insurgents in both combat and the use of sophisticated hardware and weapons. There are 1,089,700 active paramilitary personnel (including police) and 1,027,000 voluntary reserves. The Ministry of Home Affairs controls the Central Reserve Police Force (CRPF; 167,400 active); Assam Rifles (52,500); Border Security Force (BSF; 174,000); Indo-Tibetan Border Police (ITBP; 32,400); and National Security Guard, which is composed of elements of the armed forces, CRPF, and BSF (NSG; 7,400). Other paramilitary forces include the Central Industrial Security Force (95,000), Special Protection Group (3,000), Special Frontier Force (9,000), Defence Security Corps (31,000), Railway Protection Forces (70,000), and Coast Guard (more than 8,000 with 34 patrol craft). Voluntary forces include the Home Guard (574,000) and Civil Defence (453,000). Voluntary forces typically have little military training and are used for civil disturbances and relief work.

Police: As of October 2002, there were 1,015,416 police officers in India for a national average of 1 police officer per 125 persons. Police are under the control of state governments, and, with central government permission, states are allowed to create police reserve battalions; all 13 reserve police battalions are in insurgent-prone northeastern states. State police are often assisted by—and some say depend upon—paramilitaries and the armed forces for the maintenance of internal security. An August 2000 government report on police reforms suggested that the Indian police should improve their relations with civilians, place a higher priority on crime prevention, and obtain improved infrastructure. The previous review of the nation's police was conducted in the late 1970s, and its recommendations are as yet unimplemented.

Internal Threats and Terrorism: India's top security concerns are mostly internal. Indeed, much of the national security apparatus is directed to maintaining territorial integrity as dozens of groups push for varying degrees of political or social autonomy, sometimes violently. India treats separatism with extreme concern given the possibility that successful separatism may establish a precedent that other groups might seek to follow. Internal threats can be categorized as religiously oriented conflict or ethnic violence, usually with separatist objectives. The 10-year Khalistani separatist conflict in Punjab terminated in 1994, but separatist violence periodically escalates in Indian-controlled Jammu and Kashmir. Numerous separatist insurgent groups are active in the northeast, and India has periodically expanded its military efforts in Assam against groups such as the United Liberation Front of Assam (ULFA), National Democratic Front of Bodoland (NDFB), and Bodo Security Force (BSF). Other rebel groups in Assam observe cease-fire agreements with the government. The decades-long separatist conflict in Nagaland continues with the National Socialist Council of Nagaland-Khapland (NSCN-K), although peace talks have occurred with another faction, the NSCN-IM (Isaac Muivah), after the government lifted its previous ban on the organization. In Tripura, various insurgents continue to target Bengali immigrants and Indian security forces.

Religiously oriented violence has occurred, principally among Hindus and Muslims and most notably in Ayodyha (in Uttar Pradesh) and urban areas of Gujarat and Maharashtra. While less common than separatist violence, these conflicts prompt greater popular debates on Indian history, society, and politics; there are allegations that national and state-level politicians with the Bharatiya Janata Party (BJP) have facilitated such conflicts.

Human Rights: Although human rights problems exist in India, the country is generally not regarded as among the world's serious human rights violators. Human rights problems appear to be acute in areas and periods of communal violence, and security forces, insurgents, and various ethnic-based groups have all been accused of human rights violations in Jammu and Kashmir, Gujarat, Maharashtra, Uttar Pradesh, and various northeastern states. Furthermore, Hindu organizations have been accused of attacking religious minorities—particularly Muslims and Christians—and of receiving deferential treatment and even outright support from some political parties. Both international human rights organizations and India's National Human Rights Commission have questioned the impartiality of police and judicial authorities in various locales.

On the other hand, human rights groups have praised India's September 2004 repeal of the 2002 Prevention of Terrorism Act, which both the newly elected government and international organizations criticized as enabling human rights abuses by security forces. Indian media routinely address controversial issues, such as political corruption and discrimination against women, sexual minorities, indigenous peoples, and "untouchables." However, the government has been accused of harassing and jailing journalists who investigate topics such as corruption and the situation in Kashmir. Moreover, in response to cyber-crime and cyber-terrorism perpetrated by parties in both India and Pakistan, India passed the Information Technology Act of 2000, which allows cybercafés and Internet users' homes to be searched without warrants at any time as part of criminal investigations.

www.ingramcontent.com/pod-product-compliance
Lightning Source LLC
Chambersburg PA
CBHW080402290526
45790CB00009BA/3664